JUST IMAGINE!

Escape!

Tamim Ansary

Illustrations by Derrick Williams

1   2   3   4   5   6   7   8   9   10

ISBN 0-8250-4972-X

Copyright © 2004

Walch Publishing

P. O. Box 658 • Portland, Maine 04104-0658

walch.com

Printed in the United States of America

WALCH PUBLISHING

Escape!

Table of Contents

Escape!

Introduction

Suppose you fell out of an airplane. What would you do? Or suppose you were hanging from a rooftop by your ankles. Would you panic? What if you were trapped by an entire army that wanted you dead? Would you give up?

This book is about six people who did not give up. They got into some tight spots—*really* tight spots. They got into situations that seemed to have no way out. Most people would have said, "It's over. There is no escaping this one. Why even try?"

These six people did not stop trying. All six lived to tell the tales of their escapes.

Escape!

As you read about these amazing men and women, imagine yourself in their shoes. Figure out what you would do—if you can think of a plan at all. See if that's the plan they followed. What did it take to make each escape a success? Did luck play a part? Did courage come into it? What about staying cool?

The next time you feel trapped, think about these six people. Are you any more trapped than they seemed to be? Perhaps, like them, you are not really trapped. Perhaps you are just in a tight spot and escape is possible—if you stay cool, believe in yourself, and keep trying.

The Master of Escape

A black car raced through the streets of Boston. On Tremont Street, it had to slow down. The crowd was too thick.

The Master of Escape

The slender man obeyed. The guards wrapped the sleeves around his body twice. Then they tied the sleeves together behind his back. Again, they braced against the man's back to pull hard. When they were done, he could barely breathe.

Over 20,000 people had gathered on the streets below. They held their breath as they watched. Why were the guards doing this? No one can escape from a straitjacket, even from a loose one. How dangerous could this slender man be? Did they really *have* to pull the straps so tight?

No, they didn't. The slender man was not insane. He was putting on a show. His

name was Harry Houdini. In the year 1921, he was one of the world's most famous performers.

Nowadays, many people call Houdini a "magician." That was not the title he used. Houdini called himself an escape artist.

His real name was Erich Weiss. Early in his career, he did perform magic tricks on stage. That's when he took the name Harry Houdini. He was honoring a famous French magician, Robert Houdin. Harry Houdini was pretty good at stage magic. Once he made a 10,000-pound elephant disappear on stage.

Around 1908, however, he decided to

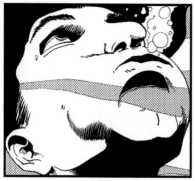

stop doing ordinary magic tricks. His greatest talent lay in escape acts. Houdini boasted that he could pick any lock—and he proved it. He could untie any rope, he said. He proved that, too. He could open any pair of handcuffs—while wearing them. He did so, on stage. Lock makers came out of the audience with handcuffs Houdini had never before seen. They all thought their handcuffs could not possibly be opened without a key. Houdini proved them wrong.

Once, he was put into the country's most

secure prison cell. Some of America's most dangerous criminals had been kept in the so-called "death cell." No one had ever escaped. Houdini had himself locked into that cell one night. In the morning, he was found outside it, calmly reading a paper!

Still, a prison cell is one thing. A straitjacket is quite another. In *this* straitjacket, Houdini couldn't even wriggle a finger. And the jacket alone was not enough of a challenge. Houdini signaled someone above. The crowd looked up and gasped. A rope was being lowered from the roof of the five-story building. The rope came over a pulley fixed to a beam. The beam held the rope away from the building.

his arms boneless, like strands of fat spaghetti?

The crowd held its breath. Houdini's hands were behind his back now, doing something to those straps. Then suddenly— the straitjacket fell off. Houdini had done it again!

"The time?"

"Twelve-forty," the tall man announced.

Houdini had escaped from a straitjacket in less than three minutes. A crowd of 20,000 had watched it happen. Not one them could say how he'd done it.

In fact, no one ever explained how Houdini managed his escapes. Oh, there was

talk of needles hidden under his eyelids. Some said he could work lock picks with his tongue. There were rumors that his skin itself was a muscle. It was all just talk.

Houdini himself never told. The world's greatest escape artist died in 1926—on Halloween night. When he died, his secrets went with him to the grave.

Danger in the Sky

Today, flying is the safest way to travel. Millions of people board airplanes every day. Ninety years ago, however, only daredevils climbed into flying machines. Airplanes had just been invented. The best ones were little more than winged motorcycles. Every safe landing in an airplane was a narrow escape from death.

One of the bravest flying daredevils was Charles Lindbergh. He was the first person to fly across the Atlantic Ocean. In 1927, he flew from New York to Paris in a tiny plane, alone. That's what most people remember about Lindbergh today.

By the time he crossed the Atlantic, however, Lindbergh was already a veteran pilot. Even as a youngster, he made his

living doing airplane stunts. Later, he flew for the post office, carrying mail from city to city. This job took great nerve. The mail pilots vowed to deliver the mail on time. They took pride in flying in every kind of weather.

Flying at night was the most dangerous part of the job. Planes had no fancy instruments then. Pilots found their way by sight. They followed roads and looked for landmarks such as hills. They learned to recognize towns along their route from the air.

At night, roads and landmarks were hard to see. Electricity being new, even

airports had few lights. Workers used flashlights to guide pilots down.

On the night of September 16, 1926, Charles Lindbergh survived the most dangerous moment of his career. He was flying from St. Louis to Chicago with stops in Springfield and Peoria. Everything was going well. He left Peoria at 5:15 P.M. It was getting dark and there was no moon, but the air was clear. Lindbergh could use the stars as guides.

Then he flew into a thick fog. It grew so dense, he could not see the ground below or the stars above. In fog like this, mail pilots were supposed to land and let

a train carry the mail the rest of the way. But where should Lindbergh land? Where was he now? He could hardly see the ground.

He dropped a flare, hoping to light up the landscape. The flare failed for some reason. It disappeared into the darkness like a stone.

Lindbergh peered into the fog and saw a dim glow, far away. Was it a town? Which town? It didn't matter. Lindbergh had been in the air too long now. He had to land somewhere—anywhere—before he

ran out of fuel.

Just then his engine died. Lindbergh heard nothing but wind hissing over his wings. He had run out of fuel. As soon as his plane lost speed, it would drop like a brick.

Luckily Lindbergh had a parachute— all pilots did. He pointed his plane toward the open countryside. That way, when it crashed, it would not hit anyone. Then he crawled onto one of the wings. Once he got past the propeller he jumped backward, clear of the plane

He counted to five and pulled the cord. Poof! His parachute opened above him

like a great white umbrella. The parachute cords jerked taut. He was floating.

Then he heard a sound. It was an airplane engine. What plane could be flying in this fog? It sounded like it was coming his way. Would the pilot see him in time?

A moment later he saw it. His heart went cold. The plane hurtling through the fog was his own. Somehow the engine had started up again. The plane was flying without a pilot. There was no one in the cockpit to see him.

Much later, he figured out what must have happened. A bit of gas must have

remained at the back of the tank. When the plane began to go down, the gas flowed forward. It poured into the engine and got it going again.

Now, the plane was flying in a big spiral, moving slowly down. Lindbergh was floating down, too. By the time the plane crossed his path, it would be at his level. Lindbergh's own plane was about to crash into him!

Frantically, he tugged at his parachute cords. If he could tilt the parachute, a wind might catch it. With luck, he would drift out of the airplane's path.

But luck was not with him. There was

no wind on this foggy night.

And now it was too late. The plane was coming. Lindbergh winced. The noise rose to a scream. Then it began to fade. Lindbergh opened his eyes. The plane had passed to his right. He laughed with relief. It was gone now, into the fog.

But it was flying in a circle and would come back around. Next time it passed, his plane would be lower—but Lindbergh would be lower, too. In the awful silence, he could hear his own heartbeat. The sound was born again. It sounded like a distant fly . . . then a bee, then a wasp, then an angry hornet. Soon it took shape

The Good Person

No one paid much attention to little Gladys Aylward. The tiny woman came from a poor family. She had never gotten much schooling. In 1930, she was working as a maid in London.

Then, one night, she heard about Jeannie Lawson. Old Mrs. Lawson worked as a missionary in China. She was looking for a younger woman to help her.

Gladys made a decision that changed her whole life. She quit her job. She set off across Russia by train. She took a boat from there to China. She kept going, by train, then bus, and then mule. At last she reached the city of Yangchen, deep in the mountains. There, she met with Mrs. Lawson.

The two women set up an inn. They

gave travelers food and shelter at a fair price. In the evening, they told their guests religious stories. After a year, Mrs. Lawson died, but Gladys went on running the inn.

One day, Gladys found a hungry child on the street. The little girl had no parents. She was covered with sores. Gladys took her in. Some months later, that girl brought home a little boy, another homeless orphan. "Can he have some food?" she asked.

And what could Gladys do? She took the boy in, too.

By 1938, she was taking care of a

hundred orphans! That year, war broke out. Japan sent armies into China. Japanese planes dropped bombs on Chinese cities. In Yangchen, the bombs killed hundreds. Many people fled the city. But then the Japanese army surrounded Yangchen and blocked all the roads. They turned Yangchen into one big prison.

The city leader gathered the people. He told them to hide from the Japanese soldiers in the mountains. Gladys would not leave. "I can't abandon my orphans," she said. "Why should the Japanese harm me? I am no danger to anyone."

The Good Person

Then someone showed her a Japanese "wanted" poster with her face on it. Under her face were words written in Chinese. They read: "Wanted dead or alive." The Japanese didn't care that Gladys was harmless. She was English—and they were at war with England as well as with China.

Gladys had no choice. If she was killed, the orphans would die, too. She had to get those children to safety. But where could she take them? The nearest orphanage was in Sian Province, 100 miles away. It lay on the other side of some rugged mountains. How could Gladys lead 100 children over those bare peaks? What would they eat? Where would they sleep?

Gladys had no answers. She only knew that they could not stay where they were. Since the roads were blocked, they had to take their chances in the mountains. She gathered the children and explained what they must do. "This journey will be hard," she warned. "We must all stay cheerful, have faith, and try our best."

Then they set out. Just as they reached the slopes, shots rang out. Japanese soldiers had spotted them leaving. Gladys wadded up her coat and held it over her head. She herded the children into hiding.

When she put her coat back on, it was full of bullet holes.

The group could not stop. Airplanes would be coming to drop bombs. But Gladys could not make the children move fast either. They were all carrying heavy bundles of food. They had to stop and rest every few minutes. That first day, the group barely covered two miles.

Each day, however, the bundles grew lighter. That's because they were eating the food. With lighter loads, they could

walk faster. But they ate less and less each day, to make the food last. Then, hunger slowed them down. And, finally, the food ran out. They had to start living off the land.

Every so often, Gladys heard the buzzing of airplanes. At that sound, she always made the children hide. She sent them crawling behind bushes and rocks. If there was no hiding place, she had them lie down and cover themselves with dirt.

It worked. The Japanese flew overhead many times. But they never spotted Gladys and the orphans.

On the twelfth day, the group came to

the Yellow River. That river is so big, it looks like a sea. From one bank, you cannot even see the other bank. In normal times, it is full of boats. On that day, no traffic moved over the water. People were staying home because of the war. They were keeping their boats hidden from the Japanese.

"Why don't we cross?" the children clamored.

"We have no boat," said Gladys sadly.

"What will we do?"

Gladys thought hard. "Sing," she said finally. So the children kneeled by the river and sang hymns. A hundred little

voices can make loud music. A Chinese army officer heard them. He came over to see who was singing. He was surprised to see a tiny English woman and a hundred Chinese children. When Gladys told him her story, he said, "Wait here."

The officer came back in an hour with a boat. It belonged to the Chinese army. That boat carried Gladys and her hundred orphans safely across the mighty Yellow River.

They kept going for another fifteen days. Some nights they found barns to sleep in. Some nights, they had to shiver under the stars. They found wild berries to

eat at times. Often, however, they went hungry.

Twenty-seven days after leaving Yangchen, they reached the orphanage in Sian. They had done it—they had escaped the Japanese army!

Inside, Gladys tottered and fell over. She was suffering from typhus fever. She had caught this terrible illness during the march. But she had not let it show. She had hidden her illness so the children wouldn't lose heart.

Gladys recovered from the illness, but she was never the same. In 1947, she returned to England. The Chinese,

however, never forgot her. There, she is still known by the name the Chinese gave her: Ai-weh-deh.

It means "The Good Person."

The moon was full that night—but so what? There was nothing to see from the top of Hill 488 except jungle. A jungle full of soldiers. You could hear them, all right. But you could not see a single one in that thick brush.

Sergeant Jimmie Howard put his mouth close to the radio. "Get us out of here," he whispered. "We're surrounded."

The voice on the radio replied, "Sorry, Jimmie. We can't get a helicopter out to you at this hour. It's too dark. You'll have to hold out till morning. We'll be there at first light."

Jimmie shut his eyes for a moment. He was sitting on a bare hilltop in Vietnam. Hundreds of enemy soldiers were moving in from all sides. What were his chances

of living through the night? Probably zero. He had only seventeen men. Fifteen were marines, like Jimmie. Two were navy men. But all were young and green. None of them had been tested in battle. They were depending on their leader. And that leader was Jimmie.

Jimmie Howard was no stranger to fighting. He had joined the Marine Corps at the age of twenty-one. He had won medals for bravery in the Korean War—a Silver Star and two Purple Hearts. Now it was 1966. Sixteen years had passed. During those years, Jimmie had learned a lot about war. But had he learned enough? Could anyone know enough to survive *this* situation? Eighteen men against hundreds?

Things looked hopeless, but Jimmie was a soldier. He followed orders. Today, his orders had him crouching on top of Hill 488. He and his men had been dropped here on June 13. They were told to watch the countryside around the hill. From the top of that hill, they could see the enemy troops moving around. They reported what they saw to pilots flying overhead. The pilots used this information to strike at enemy targets.

By the third day, however, the enemy knew someone was watching them. They

knew someone was telling the American pilots where to drop their bombs. They figured out where that someone had to be sitting. That's when the enemy troops began moving toward Hill 488.

Jimmie knew they were coming. He could see the brush moving. A few times, he caught a shadowed glimpse of an actual person. Once, he saw moonlight glinting off metal.

Then shots began to ring out. Bullets came zinging from every side. The jungle lit up in a hail of gunfire. That's when Jimmie called the base on his radio. And that's when he learned there would be no

rescue that night.

His men, meanwhile, were shooting back. Jimmie told them to stop. "There is no point shooting at trees. We have to make every bullet count. Don't shoot until you see someone."

Then, one of his men threw a grenade. A grenade is a small bomb, about the size of a baseball. The grenade exploded in the brush. The enemy soldiers hiding in that clump of brush burst out into the open. Now, suddenly, Jimmie's men could see the enemy. Shots thundered in the night.

Then silence fell. Jimmie knew it would not last. Already, the brush was

rustling. More
soldiers were creeping up the hillside on
their stomachs. "Throw more grenades,"
Jimmie ordered.

"We can't," said one of his men.
"We're all out, Sarge."

At that moment a voice came from the
thicket below. "Americans!" it growled.

Escape from Hill 488

"You have one hour to live. One hour!"

A chill ran through Jimmie. He felt the same chill run through his men. And that in itself was a new danger. Fear is the soldier's worst enemy. When frozen with fear, a soldier starts to make mistakes.

Then suddenly Jimmie knew what to do. "Laugh," he ordered. "Laugh hard."

Eighteen men started laughing. They made the night ring with their hoots and howls. Jimmie felt the tables turning. Now, it was the men hiding in the jungle who tasted fear. The Americans were outnumbered and doomed. How could they be laughing? It made no sense. Did they have some secret weapon?

Jimmie had another idea. It was a strange idea. It was so strange it almost made him laugh. But it was worth a try. "Throw rocks," he said.

"Rocks, Sarge?"

"Rocks!" Jimmie hissed.

He didn't have to say it again. His men understood. Their only hope lay in flushing the enemy out of hiding. Grenades would do that job, but they were out of grenades. In the dark, however, rocks can look just like grenades. If they look the same, they might do the same exact job.

Quietly, the men heaped up rocks the size of baseballs. When all were ready, Jimmie gave the order. His men flung rocks into the air. Dark chunks were visible against the moonlit sky. Once again, Jimmie's idea worked! The enemy soldiers burst out of hiding in a panic.

Fierce fighting followed. Within minutes, Jimmie's men had driven the enemy troops back down the hillside. Stillness fell over the jungle again.

Jimmie and his men were now running out of ammunition. They were outnumbered twenty to one. They were wounded. If the enemy attacked now,

there was nothing more they could do. They were helpless.

But the enemy did not know how helpless they were. The enemy knew only that these were men who laughed at danger. And so they stayed hidden in their bushes.

Dawn washed into the sky. The longest night of Jimmie's life ended. Six of his men lay dead. All the other men were wounded. Jimmie himself had taken a bullet in the back. He could not move his legs. But at least the rescue helicopter was coming.

Twelve men escaped death that night.

Escape from Hill 488

Later, at the base, they counted their bullets. They had only eight rounds left! That meant they could have gone on fighting for about eight more seconds! Those twelve survivors beat nearly impossible odds—and it was all thanks to Sergeant Jimmie Howard.

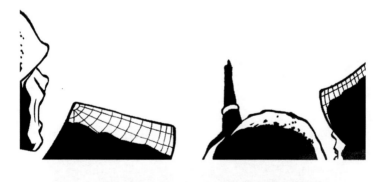

enry Brown woke up feeling sad. Six months had not softened the pain. His wife was gone and his children, too. All three had been sold to a man in another state.

"Sold? How can a human being be sold?" you may ask. Well, in 1849, in Virginia, this was not even unusual. Back then, in America's southern states, white people could own Africans as slaves. Henry Brown was property. He was born on a plantation. When his owner died, the man's son inherited Henry like a piece of furniture. He moved Henry to Richmond to work in his tobacco factory.

There in the city, Henry met his wife Nancy. She too was a slave. When she got set to marry Henry, her master promised

never to sell her. He said he believed in keeping families together. But he broke his promise. Now, Henry knew he would never see his wife and children again.

Henry often dreamed of breaking loose. He dreamed of escaping to the north, where slavery was against the law. Every slave had such dreams.

But escaping from slavery was hard and dangerous. Black people traveling alone in the south were sure to be stopped. Runaway slaves could not let themselves be seen. Therefore, they could not buy food. They could not stay in hotels, board trains, or walk the roads. They had to

travel at night, moving through swamps and woods. They had to eat whatever they could find. And some white people made their living catching escaped slaves. The slave-catchers had dogs and guns.

Henry once met a storekeeper who had helped several slaves escape. He said he could help Henry, too. He suggested several ways Henry might try to get away. But Henry didn't think any of those plans would work.

Now, he thought about that storekeeper again. At the factory, that day, he watched another slave being whipped. The boss lashed this man's back a hundred times

for working too slowly. Henry had never been whipped, but it could happen to him, too. It could happen any time. Slaves had no control over their lives.

That day, a package came for the boss. Henry watched him push the big box into his office. Suddenly, a plan blazed in Henry's mind. It was so simple, he wanted to laugh. It was so daring, he trembled. It was a strange plan! Could it possibly work?

Henry's idea was this: mailing himself to freedom. He thought of having himself shipped to the north in a crate.

He went to see the storekeeper. The

storekeeper just shook his head. "That's crazy," he said. "You'll die! But if you want to try it, I'll help you—for eighty-six dollars."

Henry handed over the money. It was half of all the money he had in the world—his life's savings. The next morning, before dawn, he went to the store. The crate was ready. It was 3 feet long, 2 feet wide, and 2 1/2 feet high. Henry was 5 feet 8 inches. He had to curl up to fit inside. He took a flask of water in with him.

The storekeeper nailed down the lid. Three tiny holes drilled into the lid let in air. On the lid was written, "This side up." The storekeeper addressed the box to William Johnson, a friend of his in Philadelphia. Then he took the crate to the Adams Express office.

From there, the box was put on a wagon—upside down! It was hauled to the train station. At the station, no one handled the box with care. Workers tossed it roughly into the baggage car. They

banged boxes around, making them fit. Henry ended up under a pile of other crates. It was hot and dark in there. He felt buried alive.

The train took the crate to the docks, where it was loaded onto a ship. Again, workers ignored the label that said "This side up." They set the crate so Henry was upside down. The blood flowed into his head. His eyes swelled up. His veins bulged.

Luckily, two men pushed the crate over to make a seat. They set Henry right side up just in time. But now the men were sitting on the box. Henry didn't dare

to wiggle. If he made the slightest noise the men would hear him. After all, he could hear them. And here's what he heard one of them say: "What's in this crate?"

Henry's heart began to pound.

After a silence, the other man said, "Just mail, probably."

Henry relaxed—as much as he could, anyway, curled up in the tiny crate.

The ship reached Washington, D.C. From there, it was supposed to go to Philadelphia by train. At the station, however, Henry heard more frightening words: "There's no more room on today's

train. Let's send this one tomorrow."

Tomorrow! Henry couldn't last that long! The heat was over 100 degrees in that crate. He could barely breathe. By tomorrow, he'd be dead.

"But it's marked 'express,'" said another voice. "We'd better get it on tonight's train, somehow."

Henry was saved! At 7:00 P.M., he reached Philadelphia. He heard horses and voices as the crate was carried through the streets. At last, with a bump, the box came to rest. Where was he now? He held his breath.

Outside the crate, a group of men had

gathered. They were William Johnson and his friends. They were expecting this "package." They knew what was in it. But hearing no sound, they feared the worst.

Inside, Henry kept still. He was taking no chances.

Finally, Johnson tapped on the lid. "Is everything all right in there?"

Then came the weak voice, "All right, sir."

Johnson ran for a crowbar and pried off the lid. Henry unfolded himself from the box. He had been in the crate for 27 hours. Another night might have killed him. But his gamble had paid off. He was

in Philadelphia—a free man at last.

And after that, for the rest of his life, people knew him as Henry "Box" Brown—in memory of his amazing escape from slavery.

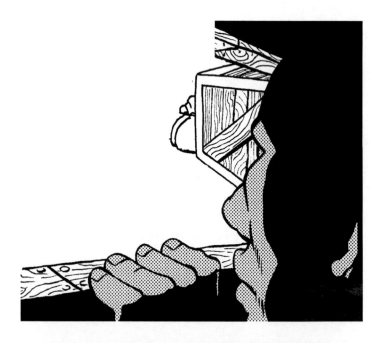

Even today, the Tower of London is a scary place—and it is only a museum. For centuries, however, it was England's darkest prison. Back then, the mere name frightened people.

The Tower isn't actually just one tower. It's a group of stone castles surrounded by a huge stone wall. The main gate faces the city. On the other side, the Thames River laps against the outer wall. An iron gate opens right into the water. Boats can sail into the prison directly from the river.

In the old days, many prisoners came in through this gate. They were brought in at night, when no one was looking. That's because the Tower was never for ordinary criminals. It was a special prison for

enemies of the king. Some were folks who had spoken or plotted against their ruler. Many, however, had done nothing at all. They were simply people the king didn't trust.

Only a few people ever tried to escape this place. One man, for example, made it as far as the river. Guards shot him full of arrows before he could swim twenty yards. Such was the fate of most prisoners who tried to escape. They died trying.

One exception was William, Earl of Nithsdale. Lord Nithsdale did not use a rope. He didn't swim across the river. He did not even come up with a plan. All

credit for his amazing escape must go to his wife, Winifrede.

The year was 1715. England had just been through a revolution. The English had kicked out their old king. A new king and queen, William and Mary, had taken the throne.

Some people, however, remained loyal to the old king. A group of these lords plotted against the new king. Their plot was discovered. Seven men were arrested and sent to the Tower of London. Six were part of the plot. The seventh was Lord Nithsdale.

Lord Nithsdale had never actually

joined the rebels. He just knew them all and lived near them. That was enough for the king. He decided to have Lord Nithsdale killed, just to be on the safe side.

Winifrede was shocked to hear of her husband's arrest. She boarded a coach at once, to follow him. Halfway to London, the coach broke down in a snowstorm. Lady Nithsdale ordered a horse and kept going. She got to London after midnight. Somehow she found a room at a boarding house.

The next morning, she went to see the king. The guards would not let her into

the palace. She spotted a lord she knew. "Please," she croaked, pressing a letter into his hand. "Give this to the king for me!"

The lord agreed to do so. The letter begged for William's life. It explained what kind of man Lord Nithsdale was. Winifrede wrote that William knew nothing about politics. He loved songs and jokes. He was a silly man, really—and no danger to anyone.

After that, Winifrede went to the Tower to see William. The guards let her in because they felt sorry for her. On the

way in, Winifrede studied the walls and halls. She counted the soldiers at the doors. She noted the size of the locks. She began to lose hope.

Back at the boarding house, bad news awaited her. The king had read her letter. He was not impressed. He had ordered that William's head be chopped off the very next morning.

That's when a plan occurred to Winifrede. She gathered four women from the boarding house and told them her idea. They agreed to help her.

The five women went to the Tower right away. Winifrede told the guards she

wanted to say goodbye to her husband. She and her friends were let in.

All five women were wearing wigs. It was the fashion then. One woman, however—Mrs. Mills—had a super large wig. The guards didn't think this odd. What did they know about fashion? They thought huge wigs must be in style.

Actually, Mrs. Mills was wearing two wigs. She had another secret, too. Under her clothes, she was wearing a second outfit!

The women found Lord Nithsdale sitting gloomily by the window. His eyes were red. He was combing his fingers

through his beard. Lady Nithsdale put a towel around his neck and began to cut his beard.

"What the—" Lord Nithsdale spluttered.

"Ssh." Lady Nithsdale put her fingers to her lips. "No time for questions."

Meanwhile, Mrs. Mills took off her outer clothes. Under the purple gown, she was wearing a brown gown.

Winifrede finished shaving William's chin. "Put on the dress," she said.

"I certainly will *not!*" William huffed.

"Would you rather wear a dress tonight

or lose your head tomorrow?" said Winifrede.

William put on the dress. Then, he let Mrs. Mills cram that extra wig onto his head.

"Let's go," said Lady Nithsdale.

She led the way. After her came Mrs. Hartfield, then Lord Nithsdale (dressed as a woman), and then Mrs. Holly. Lady Nithsdale paused to say a few words to the guard. "You have been very kind," she said, as the others swept on past. "Here are a few coins for you."

While the guard was accepting the money, Mrs. Mills came out of the prisoner's room. The guard suspected nothing. He never counted the women. He saw a bunch go in and a bunch come out. He never realized five had gone in, but six had come out.

Mrs. Mills and Lady Nithsdale hurried to the front gate. By that time, Lord Nithsdale and the others had left. A carriage had taken them away. Now, a second carriage took Mrs. Mills and Lady Nithsdale to safety.

The next morning, the guards came for Lord Nithsdale. They found his room empty. The fun-loving lord was already on the high seas by then. He and his wife

were on their way to Italy. There, they lived the rest of their days—poor but happy.